Rosa Parks

A Photo-Illustrated Biography

by Muriel L. Dubois

Consultant:
Thomas J. Davis, Ph.D., J.D., Professor
Department of History and College of Law,
Arizona State University

Bridgestone Books
an imprint of Capstone Press
Mankato, Minnesota

Bridgestone Books are published by Capstone Press
151 Good Counsel Drive, P.O. Box 669, Mankato, Minnesota 56002
http://www.capstone-press.com

Library of Congress Cataloging-in-Publication Data
Dubois, Muriel L.
    Rosa Parks / by Muriel L. Dubois.
    v. cm. (A photo-illustrated biography)
    Includes bibliographical references (p. 23) and index.
    Contents: A woman for civil rights—Rosa's early years—Growing up in Alabama
Hard work—Marriage—Rosa stays put—The bus boycott—Working for civil rights—
Honoring her work—Fast facts about Rosa Parks—Dates in Rosa Parks' life.
    ISBN 0-7368-1607-0 (hardcover)
    1. Parks, Rosa, 1913—Juvenile literature. 2. Parks, Rosa, 1913—Pictorial works
Juvenile literature. 3. African Americans—Alabama—Montgomery—Biography—Juvenile
literature. 4.Civil rights workers—Alabama—Montgomery—Biography—Juvenile
literature. 5. Montgomery (Ala.)—Biography—Juvenile literature. 6. African Americans—
Civil rights—Alabama—Montgomery—History—20th century—Juvenile literature.
7. Segregation in transportation—Alabama—Montgomery—History—20th century—
Juvenile literature. 8. Montgomery (Ala.)—Race relations—Juvenile literature. [1. Parks,
Rosa, 1913– 2. Civil rights workers. 3. African Americans—Biography. 4. Women
Biography.] I. Title.
F334.M753 P3838 2003
323'.092—dc21
    2002009491

Editorial Credits
Erika Shores, editor; Karen Risch, product planning editor; Linda Clavel, cover designer
    and interior illustrator; Alta Schaffer, photo researcher

Photo Credits
AP/Wide World Photos, cover, 16
Bettmann/Corbis, 4, 18
Corbis, 12; Jack Delano, 8; E.W. Kelley, 10; Reuters NewMedia Inc., 20
Library of Congress, 14
Photri-Microstock, 6

1 2 3 4 5 6 08 07 06 05 04 03

Table of Contents

A Woman for Civil Rights

Rosa Parks worked for civil rights. She wanted all people to be treated equally.

In 1955, Rosa lived in Montgomery, Alabama. At that time, African Americans and white Americans were segregated. Segregation kept African Americans separate from whites in many ways. In some states, African Americans went to separate schools. They used separate water fountains. African Americans could not sit with whites in restaurants or on buses.

In 1955, Rosa rode the bus home from work. The bus driver told Rosa to give her seat to a white man. When Rosa refused, she was arrested.

After Rosa's arrest, African Americans in Montgomery stopped using buses. They boycotted to show that not all Americans were treated equally. The bus boycott helped start a new interest in the fight for civil rights.

Rosa spent much of her life working for civil rights.

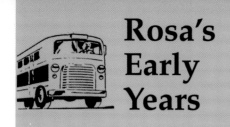

Rosa's Early Years

Rosa was born on February 4, 1913, in Tuskegee, Alabama. Her parents were James and Leona McCauley. Rosa's brother, Sylvester, was born in 1915.

James was a carpenter. Leona taught school. When Rosa was 2 years old, James left home to find work. Rosa did not see her father again until she was five. He stayed only a few days, and then he left again. Leona taught school in another town. Rosa and Sylvester lived with their grandparents.

Rosa's great-grandmother had been a slave. Rosa heard stories about slavery. She knew Abraham Lincoln freed the slaves. Rosa also knew that she was not really free. Segregation kept African Americans out of many places. They could not swim in the same pools as whites. They could not shop in some stores. African Americans often had to use different doors to enter buildings.

Segregation laws kept African Americans and whites apart.

"My grandfather was the one who instilled in my mother and her sisters, and in their children, that you don't put up with bad treatment from anybody."
–Rosa, in her book, *Rosa Parks, My Story*

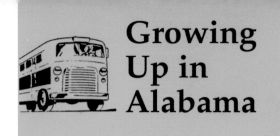

Growing Up in Alabama

Rosa often was sick as a child. She suffered from sore throats. She was small for her age. Rosa's mother decided to keep her out of school until she was six.

Rosa went to a one-room schoolhouse. Only African American children went to this school. White children had their own schools. They rode on school buses. African American children walked to school. White children sometimes threw trash at Rosa and her friends from the bus window. Rosa learned to leave the road when the bus came by.

A white boy once said he would hurt Rosa. She picked up a brick. She said she would hit him if he tried. The boy left. Rosa's grandmother was angry when she heard the story. She was afraid white people might hurt Rosa. She told Rosa to be quiet around white people. Rosa knew it was unfair that she could not stand up for herself.

These African American children went to a one-room schoolhouse similar to the one Rosa attended.

"It was hard work picking and chopping cotton. We had a saying that we worked 'from can to can't' which means working from when you can see (sunup) to when you can't (sundown)."
–Rosa, in her book, *Rosa Parks, My Story*

Hard Work

As a child, Rosa learned to work hard. Children helped plant crops in the spring. In the fall, they helped with the harvest.

Rosa and her grandparents worked their land. They had nut trees and fruit trees. They raised chickens and cows. They grew a garden. In the spring, Rosa weeded cotton plants on a neighbor's farm. In the fall, she helped pick cotton.

When Rosa was 12, a doctor removed her tonsils. Rosa missed a lot of school that year. The teachers kept her back in fifth grade. Rosa studied hard. Soon she was back with her sixth grade class.

Rosa left high school when she was 16. Her grandmother was ill. Rosa had to care for her. One month later, Rosa's grandmother died. Rosa moved to Montgomery to work in a shirt factory. She hoped to finish high school some day.

The children pictured here are working in a cotton field. As a young girl, Rosa worked in her neighbor's cotton field.

Marriage

When she was 19, Rosa married Raymond Parks. Rosa always called her husband Parks. Parks encouraged Rosa to finish school. Two years after their marriage, Rosa got her high school diploma.

Parks was an activist. He belonged to the National Association for the Advancement of Colored People (NAACP). This group worked to get equal rights for African Americans. Rosa was proud of Parks. She knew the NAACP did dangerous work. Groups such as the Ku Klux Klan did not want African Americans to have equal rights. They sometimes killed African Americans.

In 1943, Rosa joined the NAACP in Montgomery. Rosa became secretary of the Montgomery NAACP group. She went to meetings and took notes. She typed letters and wrote articles for the NAACP.

This photo shows a NAACP meeting. The group included African American and white members.

"People always say that I didn't give up my seat because I was tired, but that isn't true. I was not tired physically....I was not old....I was forty-two. No, the only tired I was, was tired of giving in."
–Rosa, in her book, *Rosa Parks, My Story*

Rosa Stays Put

One unfair law made African Americans sit in the back of public buses. African Americans had to stand if a white person needed a seat. More African Americans rode the buses than white people.

On December 1, 1955, Rosa rode the bus home after work. At one stop, some white people got on the bus. The bus seats were full. The bus driver told Rosa and other African Americans to stand. Three stood up. Rosa refused to move. The bus driver called the police to arrest her. Rosa was taken to jail.

Parks got Rosa out of jail. The NAACP wanted Rosa to go to court. They hoped the judge would decide segregation was illegal. Rosa agreed to go to court. The trial was set for Monday, December 5. The NAACP and other groups supported Rosa. The NAACP asked all African Americans in Montgomery to boycott public buses on the day of Rosa's trial.

The police took Rosa to jail for disobeying a segregation law.

The Bus Boycott

Many African Americans agreed to boycott the buses on the day of Rosa's trial. They walked to work and school. Some people with cars gave rides to the boycotters.

Dr. Martin Luther King Jr. was a minister in Montgomery. He gave many speeches about civil rights. He encouraged people to continue the bus boycott.

African Americans in Montgomery boycotted the buses through the spring, summer, and fall. Whites became upset as the boycott continued. Many whites did not think African Americans should have equal rights. Some whites threatened to hurt Rosa. Someone bombed Dr. King's house.

On November 13, 1956, the U.S. Supreme Court said segregation on public buses was against the law. African Americans waited to ride the buses until the order became official on December 20. After 381 days, the Montgomery bus boycott came to an end.

This photograph shows Rosa arriving at the court house on December 5, 1955.

Working for Civil Rights

In 1957, Rosa, Parks, and Rosa's mother, Leona, moved to Detroit, Michigan. Rosa's brother, Sylvester, lived there. He knew many white people in Montgomery were angry about the new law. He feared people would hurt Rosa.

Rosa continued to work for civil rights. She spoke all over the country. She told people about the bus boycott and segregation. African American activists sometimes held marches. They marched to support their belief in equal rights. Rosa marched with many groups.

People all over the country worked for equal rights. In 1964, Congress passed the Civil Rights Act. Segregation did not end right away. But the new law started to change African American lives. Governments could no longer make laws based on skin color.

On July 3, 1969, Rosa spoke to a crowd in front of Martin Luther King Jr.'s tomb. He was shot and killed in April 1968.

"I feel that it is better to continue to try to teach or live equality and love than it would be to have hatred or prejudice. Everyone living together in peace and harmony and love ... that's the goal that we seek....the more people there are who reach that state of mind, the better we will all be."

–Rosa, in her book, *Rosa Parks, My Story*

Honoring Her Work

Rosa received many honors for her civil rights work. The bus Rosa rode the day she was arrested drove along Cleveland Avenue in Montgomery. In 1975, Cleveland Avenue was renamed Rosa Parks Boulevard. Colleges gave Rosa honorary degrees. Troy University in Montgomery, Alabama, named their new library after Rosa.

In 1999, Congress gave Rosa the Medal of Honor. This medal is the highest award given by the U.S. government. One member of Congress said Rosa's actions "opened doors of equality for all Americans."

Rosa's work continues to help people today. Rosa believes everyone should go to school. In 1987, she started the Raymond and Rosa Parks Institute for Self Development in Detroit, Michigan. The institute is named in honor of Raymond Parks who died in 1977. The institute helps children stay in school.

This photo shows Rosa on the day she received the Medal of Honor.

Fast Facts about Rosa Parks

 Rosa was named after her grandmother Rose on her mother's side.

 Rosa Parks is called the "Mother of the Civil Rights Movement."

 Rosa was not the first person arrested for refusing to give up her bus seat to a white person. She was the first to take her case to the Supreme Court.

Dates in Rosa Parks' Life

1913—Rosa was born on February 4, in Tuskegee, Alabama.

1919—Rosa begins school.

1929—Rosa leaves high school to care for her dying grandmother.

1932—Rosa marries Raymond Parks.

1943—Rosa becomes secretary of the NAACP in Montgomery.

1955—Rosa is arrested for not giving up her seat to a white man.
　　　The Montgomery, Alabama bus boycott begins.

1956—In November, the U.S. Supreme Court states that segregation is
　　　against the law. The bus boycott ends in December.

1957—Rosa, her husband, and mother move to Detroit, Michigan.

1987—Rosa starts the Rosa and Raymond Parks Institute for
　　　Self Development.

1999—Rosa receives the Medal of Honor.

Words to Know

activist (AK-ti-visst)—a person who works to change laws

boycott (BOI-kot)—to refuse to take part in something as a way of making a protest

civil rights (SIV-il RITES)—people's rights to freedom and equal treatment under the law

equality (ee-KWOL-uh-tee)—the same rights for everyone

public (PUHB-lik)—available for all people

segregation (seg-ruh-GAY-shuhn)—the act of keeping people or groups apart

tonsils (TON-suhlz)—two flaps of soft skin on each side of the throat

Read More

Miller, William. *The Bus Ride.* New York: Lee & Low Books, 2001.

Parks, Rosa, and Gregory J. Reed. *Quiet Strength: The Faith, The Hope, and the Heart of a Woman who Changed a Nation, Reflections by Rosa Parks.* Grand Rapids, Mich.: Zondervan Publishing, 2000.

Parks, Rosa, and James Haskins. *I Am Rosa Parks.* New York: Puffin Books, 2000.

Useful Addresses

The National Civil Rights Museum
450 Mulberry Street
Memphis, TN 38103

Rosa and Raymond Parks Institute for Self Development
c/o Gregory Reed
1201 Bagley
Detroit, MI 48226

Internet Sites

Track down many sites about Rosa Parks.
Visit the FACT HOUND at *http://www.facthound.com*

IT IS EASY! IT IS FUN!

1) Go to *http://www.facthound.com*
2) Type in: 0736816070
3) Click on "FETCH IT" and FACT HOUND will find several links hand-picked by our editors.

Relax and let our pal FACT HOUND do the research for you!

Index